Social Media

Connect with a community of *Bible Studies for Life* users. Post responses to questions, share teaching ideas, and link to great blog content: **facebook.com/biblestudiesforlife.**

Get instant updates about new articles, giveaways, and more: **@BibleMeetsLife.**

The App

Simple and straightforward, this elegantly designed iPhone app gives you all the content of the Bible study book—plus a whole lot more—right at your fingertips. Available in the iTunes App Store; search **"Bible Studies for Life."**

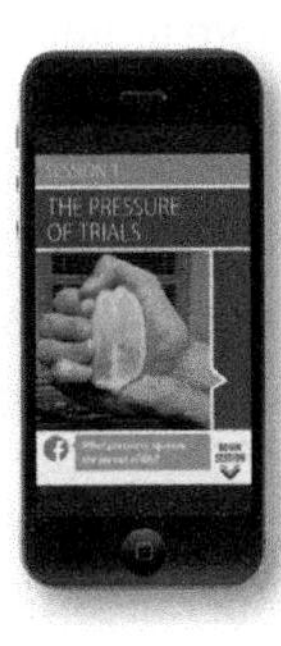

Blog

At **biblestudiesforlife.com/blog** you will find all the magazine articles we mention in this study guide and music downloads provided by LifeWay Worship. Plus, leaders and group members alike will benefit from the blog posts written for people in every life stage—singles, parents, boomers, and senior adults—as well as media clips, connections between our study topics, current events, and much more.

Training

For helps on how to use Bible Studies for Life, tips on how to better lead groups, or additional ideas for leading this session, visit **ministrygrid.com/web/biblestudiesforlife.**

Dewey decimal classification: 231.4
Subject heading: GOD—ATTRIBUTES

Eric Geiger
Vice President, LifeWay Resources

Ronnie Floyd
General Editor

David Francis
Managing Editor

Gena Rogers
Sam O'Neal
Content Editors

Michael Kelley
Director, Groups Ministry

Send questions/comments to: Content Editor, *Bible Studies for Life: Adults;* One LifeWay Plaza; Nashville, TN 37234-0152; or make comments on the web at biblestudiesforlife.com.

Printed in the United States of America

For ordering or inquiries, visit LifeWay.com; write to LifeWay Small Groups; One LifeWay Plaza; Nashville, TN 37234-0152; or call toll free 800-458-2772.

Bible Studies for Life: Adults often lists websites that may be helpful to our readers. Our staff verifies each site's usefulness and appropriateness prior to publication. However, website content changes quickly, so we encourage you to approach all websites with caution. Make sure sites are still appropriate before sharing them with students, friends, and family.

Start by believing. Then go beyond belief.

The digital age has produced huge amounts of information that have radically advanced human learning. The amount of knowledge available to us is mind-numbing. In fact, information is multiplying so rapidly that textbooks, how-to manuals, and even daily newspapers seem perpetually outdated. But what do we know about God? Are we advancing as rapidly in our knowledge of Him?

People have used the explosion of social media primarily to inform friends and others about themselves and their lives. Therefore, we know more *about* one another, but do we really *know* one another? There's a big difference between the two. The same is true when it comes to our relationship with God. We can learn more and more about God by studying His Word, but we also need to know Him in order for our lives to be changed.

That's why this study, *Beyond Belief,* is so important. *Beyond Belief* seeks to help us increase our knowledge of God by studying His character and moral attributes. But we don't want to just know about God; we want to know Him more intimately.

We could spend a lifetime studying the character and attributes of God revealed in the Bible and still only begin to scratch the surface of understanding the sovereign God of all creation. Therefore, the sessions in this study will focus on six major attributes of God: God's holiness, God's love, God's justice, God's forgiveness, God's wisdom, and God's faithfulness.

As we begin to understand what God is like and how He works in our lives, we will not only know God more, but we will also learn about ourselves and who we are in Christ.

Freddy Cardoza

Dr. Cardoza has served 20 years in full-time local-church ministry. He currently serves as the department chair of Christian ministries and the director of distributive learning at Biola University (Talbot School) in Los Angeles. He also serves as the executive director of the Society of Professors in Christian Education. Freddy has been married for 20 years to Kristin. They have two teenage sons, Dakota and Christian.

contents

SESSION 1

GOD IS HOLY

When have you seen or experienced something you would describe as one-of-a-kind?

#BSFLholy

QUESTION ***#1***

THE POINT

God's holiness calls me to be holy.

THE BIBLE MEETS LIFE

If you love walking through a museum, you're not alone. Tens of millions of people visit museums every year. What draws us to these places? Unique, novel, or beautiful items. There are museums devoted to cars, abstract paintings, Star Trek, and even asphalt.

The world's most prestigious museums also have one-of-a-kind pieces in their collections. There is after all only one *Starry Night,* one *Mona Lisa,* and one Rosetta Stone. We value these items because of their rarity, beauty, or historical significance. Some of these pieces are even considered priceless.

But what is truly beautiful is that we don't have to visit a museum to interact with something that is one-of-a-kind. What is truly beautiful is that there is only one God, and He loves His creation with a one-of-a-kind love. God alone is set apart and like no other. The Bible wraps all this up with one word: holy.

In this session we'll see that God calls us to be like Him—set apart for His glory.

WHAT DOES THE BIBLE SAY?

Psalm 99:1-9 (HCSB)

1 The LORD reigns! Let the peoples tremble. He is enthroned above the cherubim. Let the earth quake.

2 Yahweh is great in Zion; He is exalted above all the peoples.

3 Let them praise Your great and awe-inspiring name. He is holy.

4 The mighty King loves justice. You have established fairness; You have administered justice and righteousness in Jacob.

5 Exalt the LORD our God; bow in worship at His footstool. He is holy.

6 Moses and Aaron were among His priests; Samuel also was among those calling on His name. They called to Yahweh and He answered them.

7 He spoke to them in a pillar of cloud; they kept His decrees and the statutes He gave them.

8 LORD our God, You answered them. You were a forgiving God to them, an avenger of their sinful actions.

9 Exalt the LORD our God; bow in worship at His holy mountain, for the LORD our God is holy.

Key Words

Cherubim (v. 1)—Cherubim are angelic creatures who serve God. Two golden images of cherubim sat atop the ark in the most holy place of the temple.

Holy (vv. 3,5,9)—The term refers to someone or something set apart from life's common aspects. God is set above creation and is perfect in every way.

Pillar of cloud (v. 7)—God sometimes made His presence known to His people as they journeyed with a pillar of cloud. Here He spoke from such a cloud.

Psalm 99:1-3

God is not a part of it. God is neither a human nor superhuman. God is over all. He is completely and totally separate from everything or everyone we could imagine.

As human beings, we are created in God's image, which means God breathed a spirit into us. Each of us possess a spirit that was intended for a unique relationship with Him. We were created to live forever with Him. But that's where the similarity stops.

Though we are like God, God is not like us. We are created in His image; He was not created in ours. God exists independently and without reliance on any other beings or forces. God is absolutely sacred, above criticism, incorruptible, and invincible. He is holy.

Consider these elements that point to God's holiness:

- **The reign of God.** The psalmist understood the distinction, glory, and authority of royalty, and he exalted God to His rightful place. The psalmist invited others to acknowledge the reality of God's sovereign rule over all people and things.
- **The name of God.** The psalmist used God's holiest name: Yahweh. Yahweh calls attention to God as the Ancient of Days. He is the one and only God, and it was in His name and by His power that the Israelites were able to enter the land and establish their nation. Because of the holy fear the psalmist had for the awe-inspiring name of God, he called upon all of God's people to give praise, glory, and honor to the only true God.

God is truly different from us—and from anything else. And that's why we are told to praise Him. God invites us to carefully consider Him in order to discover His greatness and grandeur. When we do, we will realize that He is worthy of all praise and glory.

When was a time God's holiness became real to you?

QUESTION **#2**

PICTURING HOLINESS

Choose one of the images.
Record what it means to strive for holiness in that specific area of life.

Psalm 99:4-5

The problems of life may seem great, but they are not greater than God. There is nothing that can keep our great and awesome God from working His fairness, justice, and righteousness in our lives.

Those are three important concepts that contribute to God's holiness:

- **Fairness.** Though life isn't always fair, God is. He is the source of fairness, for He established it. Unfairness can make life feel uncertain, but because God has established fairness, Christ followers can live with confidence despite any inequities we see or experience. God will act in righteous wisdom as He oversees our lives.

Is God fair to forgive a mass murderer? Is God fair to forgive me? He is still fair in that He dealt with our sin, but He dealt with it through the death of Jesus. Grace is God's generous favor on our lives in spite of our actions. Mercy is His withholding what is fair (our punishment) in order to cover our wrong actions with compassion and forgiveness.

How does God's justice, fairness, or righteousness impact your daily routine?

QUESTION **#3**

- **Justice.** Justice occurs when God brings His divine order to life. God's justice deals out blessings and punishment. God will not let injustice stand. His holiness ensures evil will be punished and good rewarded.

- **Righteousness.** God always does what is best and what is right. Righteousness has to do with God's moral purity. His innate goodness ensures that He will always do what is right. God can always be trusted.

How should we respond to God's holiness? We "bow in worship at His footstool." The footstool was a symbol for dominion, and God is pictured as a king enthroned in heaven with the earth as His footstool. God's holiness should cause us to live with worshipful trust and submission before Him.

What do these verses teach us about a lifestyle of worship?

QUESTION **#4**

Psalm 99:6-9

We've already seen that our holy God is involved in our lives through His fairness, justice, and righteousness, but He also desires to speak into our lives. And when God speaks, He wants us to listen and respond. No matter what's happening around us or inside us, God wants us to acknowledge His presence and call on Him. He wants us to recognize His concern and that He answers us.

Because God is fair, just, and righteous, He can be totally trusted. He is the only one who deserves our complete faith. People who walked with God—people such as Moses, Aaron, and Samuel—modeled this trust. God spoke; they listened and trusted.

Like Samuel, Aaron, and Moses, our lives are filled with spiritual victories and sometimes significant defeats. God continues to reveal Himself to us in all these things, seeking to deepen our awareness of who He is and what He is like. And when we realize who God is and respond with humble hearts, He forgives us. As the priests and prophets cried out to Yahweh, He answered them and spoke to them. God works the same way today. **When we call on His name, He will meet us where we are, forgive us, and put us in a right relationship with Him.**

He may not speak to us in a pillar of cloud, but He will make Himself known. When we see God for who He is, we should respond by exalting Him and lowering ourselves. Just as the nation of Israel bowed at the holy mountain, we should humbly submit our lives to our Holy God as a worship offering.

How can we tremble at God's holiness yet still have an intimate relationship with Him?

QUESTION **#5**

LIVE IT OUT

God's holiness is not an abstract concept with no practical impact on how we live. We are called to be holy because God is holy (see 1 Pet. 1:16), so consider some practical ways to live a life of holiness:

- **Surrender.** Submit to God's holiness by placing your faith in Christ for salvation.
- **Bow in worship.** Be intentional about praising God this week. Set aside a specific period of time and worship Him in response to His holiness.
- **Unplug and listen.** Choose to abstain from one form of technology this week—social media, texts, TV, and so on. Use that time each day as an opportunity to focus on God.

As we live for the Lord, we become holy like Him. And then, like a precious work of art, we grow into a beautiful masterpiece made by God (see Eph. 2:10).

Waiting Room

I sit in the waiting room. The receptionist took my name, recorded my insurance data, and gestured to a chair. "Please have a seat. We will call you when the doctor is ready." I look around. A mother holds a sleeping baby. A woman with a newspaper looks at her watch, sighs, and continues the task of the hour: waiting. The waiting room. Not the examination room. That's down the hall. Not the consultation room. That's on the other side of the wall. Not the treatment room. Exams, consultations, and treatments all come later. The task at hand is the name of the room: the waiting room.

To continue reading "Waiting Room" from *HomeLife* magazine, visit *BibleStudiesforLife.com/articles*.

My group's prayer requests

My thoughts

SESSION 2

GOD IS LOVING

What makes you love someone?

#BSFLloving

QUESTION ***#1***

THE POINT

God's love empowers me to love.

THE BIBLE MEETS LIFE

There's power behind the throne.

Great leaders in history rarely stand alone. Whether you study ancient kings or modern movers and shakers in the business world, there is often someone (or several people) standing in the background to give advice and counsel. Such people exert a power and influence that isn't openly seen. But it *is* felt.

You may not be a king, but there is a power that motivates and influences your actions and behavior. For some of us, the "power behind the throne" comes from friends, a demanding employer, or a persistent spouse. We can also be influenced by the sway of the crowd or by slick marketing messages.

Thankfully, love may be the most potent "mover and shaker" in our lives. We discover in God a love that endures, a love that persists no matter what, and a love that always seeks our best. The Book of 1 John helps us discover the beauty of God's love—a love that is poured out on us so that His love can pour through us.

WHAT DOES THE BIBLE SAY?

1 John 4:7-12 (HCSB)

7 Dear friends, let us love one another, because love is from God, and everyone who loves has been born of God and knows God.

8 The one who does not love does not know God, because God is love.

9 God's love was revealed among us in this way: God sent His One and Only Son into the world so that we might live through Him.

10 Love consists in this: not that we loved God, but that He loved us and sent His Son to be the propitiation for our sins.

A HOLY PAY MENT

11 Dear friends, if God loved us in this way, we also must love one another.

12 No one has ever seen God. If we love one another, God remains in us and His love is perfected in us.

Key Words

Propitiation (v. 10)—This term refers to a sin offering designed to appease God's wrath against the sinner. Since God alone can forgive sin, His righteous indignation against sin must be satisfied.

Remains (v. 12)—God lives within believers. His presence is sensed as believers love one another. He remains, abides, and dwells in the hearts of those who love Him.

Perfected (v. 12)—The biblical meaning refers to something being completed, accomplished, or finished. As we walk with God, we reach His goal of loving others.

1 John 4:7-8

We were created with the capacity to love and be loved. While God has graciously given us many ways to know and experience this unconditional acceptance and affection—such as family, friends, or a spouse—our need for love is truly filled only by God Himself. God is love. And without a relationship with a loving God, we will always feel a void deep in our hearts.

It's a great gift to discover God not only has love and gives love, but that He *is* love. Whereas holiness is the fundamental characteristic of God's Person, love might be called His primary moral attribute. Love is what God is all about. God's love empowers us to love ourselves and others. That's why the apostle John exhorted us to love one another. Christians are to love other Christians because we are spiritual brothers and sisters in God's family. Our genuine love for one another indicates to others that we are God's children.

Sadly, not everyone is easy to love. Not even us! This passage teaches that our love for other believers is not something that springs out of our own natural goodness. Instead, verse 7 says we should love one another "because love is from God." For Christians, a loving spirit is a by-product of a "new birth" in Christ.

Here's how it works:

1. When we accept God's love and trust Him, He imparts His Spirit into us.

2. The Spirit of God makes us new creations.

3. It is by the presence of God's Holy Spirit that His love flows through us.

This love is not actually from us, but from God Himself. And He intends for love's transformative power to flow toward even the most despicable people—not just to those in the family of God. To make himself clear, John reiterated this truth by saying that if we don't allow God to love others through our lives, then we don't personally know Him.

How does the statement "God is love" differ from saying "God loves"?

QUESTION **#2**

"When God wanted to inform us about who He is and what He is like, He came in person."

—FREDDY CARDOZA

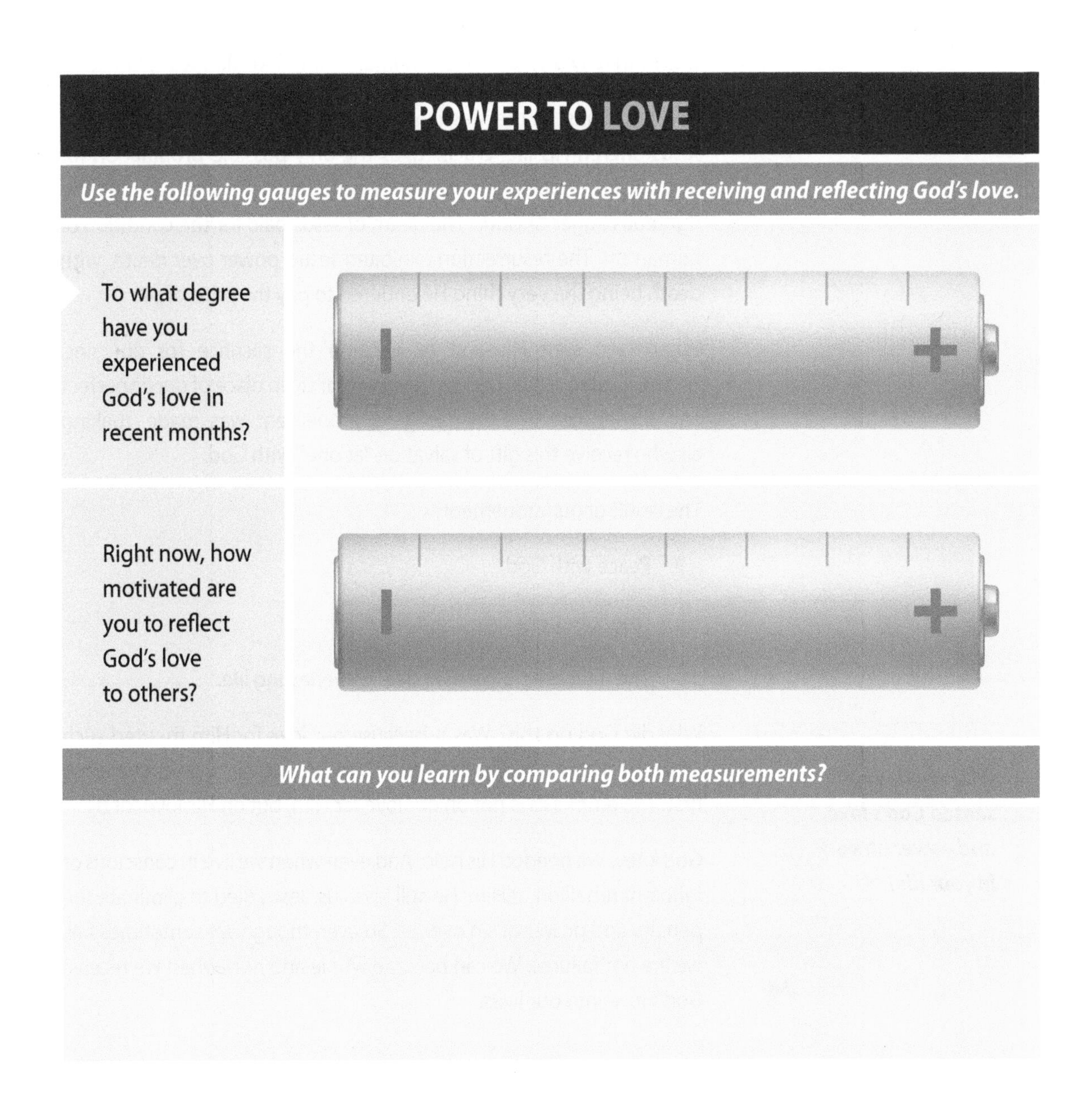

1 John 4:9-10

What do you find remarkable in verses 9-10?

QUESTION **#3**

We know about the love of God because His love was "revealed" (v. 9). It's interesting that God did not merely tell us about His love; He showed it. When God wanted to inform us about who He is and what He is like, He came in person. God came in a human body that was both fully divine and fully human—the God-Man Jesus Christ.

God sent Christ as the Messiah—the Savior of the world. As Messiah, Jesus offered His life, crucified, as the only possible propitiation for all our sins. *Propitiation* means "a holy payment that satisfies the righteous anger of God." The death of Jesus paid for the condition of human sin. The resurrection exhibited Jesus' power over death, with death being the very thing He endured to pay the price of sin.

When God sent His Son to become the sacrifice for our sins, He substituted Jesus' perfect payment for sin in place of our imperfect and inadequate one. In doing so, atonement was made, making all who receive this gift of salvation "at one" with God.

The result of our atonement?

- Peace with God
- Freedom from sin
- The ultimate power over death: everlasting life.

When have you sensed God's love and power at work in your life?

QUESTION **#4**

Why did God do this? Was it because our love for Him merited such an unspeakable gift? Hardly. Verse 10 makes it clear that God loved us first. The emphasis is not on our love for Him, but on His love for us.

God knew we needed His help. And even when we live in conscious or ignorant rebellion of Him, He still loves us. Jesus died to eliminate the penalty and power of sin over us. So even though we sometimes fail, we are not failures. We can become whole and holy when we receive God's love into our lives.

1 John 4:11-12

What is the greatest force in the universe? Scientists may point to gravity, electromagnetism, or super massive black holes—but I believe a force exists that is even greater than those: God's love.

The power of God's love gives us the ability to love the unlovely and the unlovable. Through God's love, we find the grace to unconditionally accept people whose actions are unacceptable. Of course, our unconditional love for others is no indication that we agree with their behavior, just as God's love for us is not an endorsement of the way we have sinned against Him.

This is one of the greatest truths of the Bible: God loves us. Let that truth sink in. Our lives are in trouble if our relationship with God rests primarily on us. God knows we are prone to wander. We do nothing to make God love us; He just loves us. Our response is to love Him and love those He loves. That's what verse 11 means when the apostle John gently appealed to believers as friends. He used a conditional statement: "If God loved us in this way, [then] we also must love one another." As recipients of God's love, we are obligated to love others. Because God has loved us at our worst, He has the moral authority to command us to do likewise.

God's desire is for us to live in His love and to share that same love with others. Although God Himself is invisible, He is clearly seen in our lives as we demonstrate His great love to others. The bold witness of unconditional love will draw others into an everlasting relationship with God through Christ.

How will being loved by God shape the way you live?

QUESTION ***#5***

LIVE IT OUT

How can you let God's love shape your day-to-day life?

- **Embrace God's love.** Pray specifically for God to help you understand, believe, and receive His love for you today.
- **Reflect God's love.** Before the day is over, make an effort to express love to someone in a way that mirrors God's love for you. (*Note: this experience will be most powerful if you're able to express love to someone who doesn't deserve it.*)
- **Seek reconciliation.** Identify a relationship that's been strained or broken in recent years. Let God's empowering love be the catalyst for you to request or offer forgiveness in that relationship as a step toward reconciliation.

There's definitely "power behind the throne." Let your power be God's love. Let it be the motivator in your life—the force that influences your actions and your behavior each day.

Love Is Greater Than Our Sins

I want our kids to know that in our family, we mess up, we fess up, we own up, and we make up. It's just that simple.

Love > OUR SINS

By Jen Hatmaker

My heart burns with a hot, fiery, consuming love for my son, and this lapse in judgment is so very small compared with the rest of our story together.

I want our kids to know that in our family, we mess up, we fess up, we own up, and we make up.

It's just that simple.

To continue reading "Love Greater Than Our Sins" from *HomeLife* magazine, visit *BibleStudiesforLife.com/articles*.

My group's prayer requests

My thoughts

SESSION 3

GOD IS JUST

When it comes to fighting for justice, who is your favorite character?

#BSFLjust

QUESTION #1

THE POINT

God is always just.

THE BIBLE MEETS LIFE

We love the idea of justice triumphing over injustice.

In *The Count of Monte Cristo* Edmond Dantés was a talented, handsome man of faith who was betrayed by three jealous and greedy men. Edmond was publicly declared dead even as his betrayers conspired to have him locked away in the terrible island dungeon called *Château d'If.* Worst of all, one of the betrayers later married Edmond's fiancé, Mercédès, as a way of offering comfort to her after Edmond's loss.

Where was the justice? Hopeless, bitter, and forgotten, Edmond nearly lost his faith. Punished for a crime he didn't commit, God seemed nowhere to be found. In the end, however, Edmond escaped. After many years, both he and the evil-doing trio received their just rewards.

In this session, we'll explore why we can have confidence that God's justice will always win out in the end.

WHAT DOES THE BIBLE SAY?

Ezekiel 18:21-24, 30-32 (HCSB)

21 "Now if the wicked person turns from all the sins he has committed, keeps all My statutes, and does what is just and right, he will certainly live; he will not die.

22 None of the transgressions he has committed will be held against him. He will live because of the righteousness he has practiced.

23 Do I take any pleasure in the death of the wicked?" This is the declaration of the Lord GOD. "Instead, don't I take pleasure when he turns from his ways and lives?

24 But when a righteous person turns from his righteousness and practices iniquity, committing the same detestable acts that the wicked do, will he live? None of the righteous acts he did will be remembered. He will die because of the treachery he has engaged in and the sin he has committed.

---

30 "Therefore, house of Israel, I will judge each one of you according to his ways." This is the declaration of the Lord GOD. "Repent and turn from all your transgressions, so they will not be a stumbling block that causes your punishment.

31 Throw off all the transgressions you have committed, and get yourselves a new heart and a new spirit. Why should you die, house of Israel?

32 For I take no pleasure in anyone's death." This is the declaration of the Lord GOD. "So repent and live!"

Ezekiel 18:21-23

Have you ever known someone who lived a life of excess, yet seemed to suffer no ill effects? That's the scenario that troubled the people of Judah. They saw Jerusalem lying in ruins from the Babylonian invasion. Those who survived the onslaught were forcibly taken to Babylon. The Jews cried out to God for answers.

In response, God spoke through the prophet Ezekiel. In Ezekiel 18 God candidly addressed the charge that His actions against His people were unfair. To fully appreciate this passage, let's focus on two key words:

1. **Justice.** The biblical concept of divine justice is almost perfectly captured in the statue of Lady Justice at the U.S. Supreme Court Building in Washington, D.C. Blindfolded, she holds a double-edged sword in her right hand and a set of scales in her left. The blindfold signifies her impartiality. The sword illustrates the discerning character of truth (see Heb. 4:12), and the scales represent the exacting nature of justice (see Prov. 20:23). Scripture calls God the "righteous judge" (see Ps. 7:11). As such, complaints about His fairness are unfounded. God is just.

2. **Repentance.** Repentance involves turning away from sin and committing to love and obey God. Here's the great news: any person who approaches God in this way will receive pardon. God will always act favorably and mercifully toward the one who turns to Him with a repentant heart.

Why does it sometimes bother us when someone gets let off the hook?

QUESTION **#2**

God is just in how He responds to the unrighteous who repent. Let's not miss the wonderful truth about God's character in verse 23. God doesn't enjoy punishing people—not even His enemies. He delights in seeing the wicked turn from their evil ways. God desires for all to come to repentance (see 2 Pet. 3:9).

How do these verses serve as both good news and bad news?

QUESTION **#3**

Ezekiel 18:24

After discussing the unrighteous who repent, God addressed the apparently righteous person who rebels. In this verse, God called out seemingly righteous individuals who become spiritually distracted and pursue a life indistinguishable from nonbelievers.

This scenario also points to the fairness and justice of God, even though it went against the common thinking of the Jews. The Jews were relying on their privileged heritage and past obedience to release them from divine punishment. They misunderstood what it meant to be God's chosen people and expected their special standing to free them from any consequences.

Christians possess eternal security in Christ, but that doesn't give us a free pass to sin. Believers and unbelievers alike will be held accountable for their actions. The only difference is that the believer's eternal home with Christ in heaven is never in jeopardy (see 1 Cor. 3:11-15). Once obtained, salvation is secure. But Christians certainly can (and do) suffer the same earthly consequences for their sins as those who don't know God.

The truth of eternal security should never result in taking a jaded or blasé attitude toward holy living. Sin is serious. While we sometimes fail to be controlled by the Holy Spirit and become disobedient to God, consistent sin should not characterize our lives.

God is just in how He responds to the seemingly righteous who rebel. God never produces a false verdict. He always knows all the facts, and He renders the right judgment. As such, God remains righteous and completely justified in whatever punishment and consequences He deals to the person He finds guilty. We can be assured that the approach God takes is always perfectly appropriate. Moreover, He always puts the offending person or party in the best possible position for repentance and restoration.

Why don't we take sin as seriously as we should?

QUESTION **#4**

Ezekiel 18:30-32

Ezekiel 18 helps us see two important things about God:

1. **God always gets justice right.** While earthly courts may attempt to be fair and unbiased, God's court always renders exacting, authoritative, and sound justice.

2. **God always wants our best.** His judgment is undergirded by a heart of compassion. God is not only our Judge, He is also our Defender and Mediator (see 1 Tim. 2:5-6).

All God requires is that we repent and turn from all our transgressions. When we confess our sin, God completely forgives us. That's amazing news for two reasons. First, when God forgives, He forgets. Jeremiah gave this declaration from God: "For I will forgive their wrongdoing and never again remember their sin" (Jer. 31:34).

Second, God relieves us of guilt. There is nothing more painful than a guilty conscience. Guilt can affect us spiritually, emotionally, physically, and relationally. Thankfully, a person who repents is not only set free from his or her sin, but also from the guilt associated with that sin (see Ps. 32:5). If you are forgiven, you can release the guilt that you—and others—hold over you.

Forgiveness doesn't remove the effects of our sin on either ourselves or victims of our behavior. What's done cannot always be undone. Therefore, a forgiven person takes full responsibility for the past, acknowledges his or her actions and any pain that was caused, and seeks to correct any damage caused by his or her actions as necessary. But that's where it stops. There is no obligation to bear false guilt for already-forgiven sins that Christ has paid for in full.

God is just. He dealt with your sin through the death and resurrection of Jesus Christ. And now that your sin has been dealt with, it's over. Justice is done. Furthermore, the completed justice of God means that you won't have to carry the burden of your sin any longer. You're free to live in Christ.

God is both just and forgiving. How does that combination lead to a full life for those who follow Him?

QUESTION **#5**

WHAT DO YOU SAY?

Choose one of the following statements.
How would you respond in light of what you've learned about God's justice?

"I know I'm going to heaven because I've done more good than bad."

"God can't love me because He knows what I've done."

"God acts justly from within, not in obedience to some imaginary law. He is the Author of all laws, and acts like Himself all the time."

—A. W. TOZER

LIVE IT OUT

How will you respond to God's justice?

- **Choose freedom.** Confess a specific sin or sinful pattern to God. Receive His forgiveness and choose to move forward with the knowledge that He has set you free from that sin.
- **Seek justice in the world.** Look for situations where justice seems to be lacking. Use these situations as reminders to pray that God would carry out His justice in the world.
- **Close the gap between your reputation and character.** Ask a fellow believer to hold you accountable in areas where you struggle with sin. Commit to integrity between how others know you and how God knows you.

You may be experiencing unfair circumstances in your life, but rest in the fact that God is always just and He always delivers. Whether in this life or the next, God's righteousness will triumph.

Your Kingdom Come

Your Kingdom Come

By Richard Stearns

God calls us to go into the world and change it by proclaiming the good news of His kingdom.

I'll never forget our family's first visit to Walt Disney World. My wife, Reneé, and I waited until all five of our kids were out of diapers before booking the vacation. Our youngest had turned 3, and our oldest was 16. So we bought our tickets and reserved the hotel rooms. I even picked up guidebooks on how to avoid long lines. Our first night in Orlando, Florida, we planned to visit the "Hoop-Dee-Doo Musical Revue," but on the way, our 6-year-old son, Pete, was hurt. As we walked to the venue, Pete saw a playground, ran to it, tripped, and hit his face on the first step.

To continue reading "Your Kingdom Come" from *HomeLife* magazine, visit *BibleStudiesforLife.com/articles*.

My group's prayer requests

My thoughts

SESSION 4

GOD IS FORGIVING

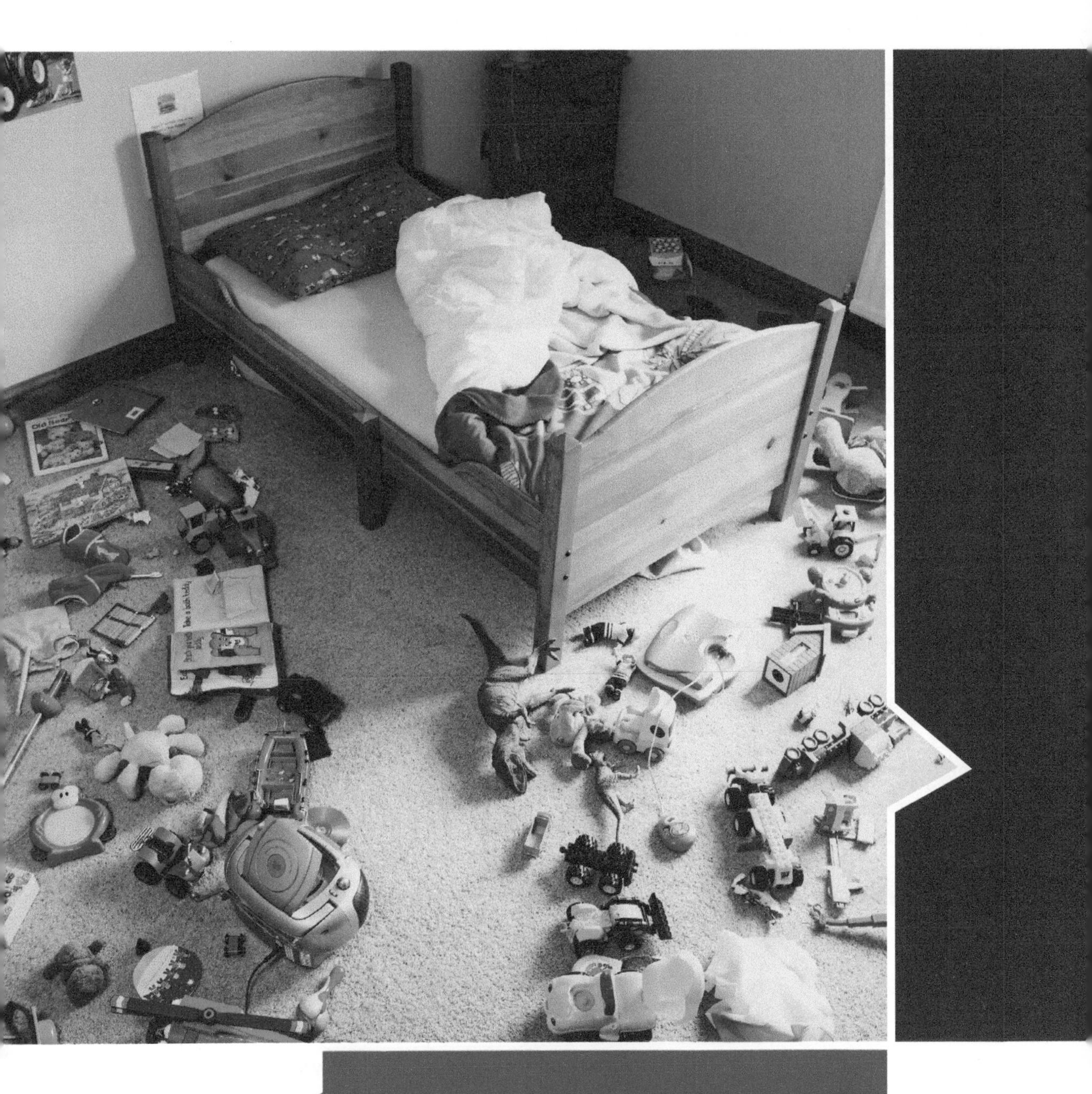

What rule did you break the most growing up?

#BSFLforgiving

QUESTION #1

THE POINT

God always forgives when I truly repent.

THE BIBLE MEETS LIFE

Sometimes forgiveness is hard—really hard.

"She walked out on our kids and our 20-year marriage to do what she wanted to do." "We trusted this advisor, and now our life savings and retirement are gone for good." "He hurt my daughter." "He opened fire in a school."

Those aren't scenarios in which we expect to hear the word "forgiveness." And why should we? Especially if the person who did wrong isn't sorry. Wouldn't forgiving such a person be the same as approving what he or she did? We can't forget. We can't trust the person any longer. So why should we forgive?

One answer to that question is to remember how much God has forgiven us. He forgives us when we walk away. He forgives us when we squander and abuse all that He has given us. He forgives us when we hurt His children—those He loves.

The short letter of 1 John shows us just how far God will go to forgive.

WHAT DOES THE BIBLE SAY?

1 John 1:5–2:2 (HCSB)

1:5 Now this is the message we have heard from Him and declare to you: God is light, and there is absolutely no darkness in Him.

6 If we say, "We have fellowship with Him," yet we walk in darkness, we are lying and are not practicing the truth.

7 But if we walk in the light as He Himself is in the light, we have fellowship with one another, and the blood of Jesus His Son cleanses us from all sin.

8 If we say, "We have no sin," we are deceiving ourselves, and the truth is not in us.

9 If we confess our sins, He is faithful and righteous to forgive us our sins and to cleanse us from all unrighteousness.

10 If we say, "We don't have any sin," we make Him a liar, and His word is not in us.

2:1 My little children, I am writing you these things so that you may not sin. But if anyone does sin, we have an advocate with the Father—Jesus Christ the Righteous One.

2 He Himself is the propitiation for our sins, and not only for ours, but also for those of the whole world.

Key Words

Fellowship (1:6)—The Greek root word means "common." This term implies that those in fellowship with one another share things in common as part of their relationship.

Advocate (2:1)—One who stands beside. The related verb means "encourage," "exhort," "counsel," or "comfort." In John's Gospel it refers to the Holy Spirit, but here to Jesus.

Propitiation (2:2)—The Greek word refers to the appeasement of God's wrath against sin through the appropriate sacrifice, which could only occur through the death of God's Son.

What evidence do you see of darkness and light in your town or community?

QUESTION #2

1 John 1:5-10

God gave our world the wonderful gift of friendship, but He gave Christians specifically the additional gift of fellowship. Fellowship goes far beyond friendship; it's tied to something that unites us in a powerful way because of what we share in common. Fellowship points to the intimate spiritual connection between Christians—a connection that exists both in and through Jesus Christ.

The opening verses of 1 John tie our fellowship with God and with His Son to the eternal life we have in Him (vv. 2-3). And here's the interesting thing: if I have eternal life and fellowship with God, and you also have it, then we have fellowship with each other. With that in mind, how do we gain this fellowship with God? How do we access it? Only through the forgiveness that is available through Christ.

John used the metaphor of "light" when writing about God. He described God as having "absolutely no darkness in Him," which is a reference to God's perfection. Only God is truly perfect, and God's perfection makes Him the embodiment of righteousness. As the Righteous One, He exists in unapproachable light.

We are not perfect. Because we have sin in our lives, we are in darkness. And if we're living in darkness, we cannot possibly be living in the light as well—not on our own. But the great news for us is that Christ removes our sin and forgives us. Consequently, He moves us away from darkness and into the light of God and fellowship with Him.

We can look at God's forgiveness in two ways. We'll call the first one "judicial forgiveness," and it occurs when God—acting as the Righteous Judge—grants us salvation.

When we submit to Jesus as our Savior, we are forgiven and declared righteous by God (see Rom. 5:6-11; Eph. 1:7). This is called justification; it's a one-time event that can never be repeated. Judicial forgiveness, then, establishes our never-ending relationship with God. Believers who trust in Christ not only escape God's wrath but are also granted everlasting life in heaven (see John 3:16) and an abundant life on earth (see John 10:10).

That brings up an interesting question: *If God forgives my sin and brings me into a relationship (fellowship) with Him, what happens if I sin again? Do I lose that relationship?* Read on.

What emotions do you experience at the thought of confessing your sin?

QUESTION #3

BARRIERS TO FORGIVENESS

HYPOCRISY
PRIDE
PEER PRESSURE
ADDICTION
APATHY
GUILT
DESIRE
REPUTATION
IGNORANCE
SHAME
STUBBORNNESS

Circle any of the above obstacles that prevent you from repenting of your sin and seeking God's forgiveness.

What's one step you can take to begin knocking down those obstacles and move toward forgiveness?

1 John 2:1-2

John wrote these truths so that we "may not sin." As Christians, we are not to live in a way that's characterized by disobedience. Still, the tendency toward sin remains powerful, and because it's embedded in our very nature, we still can—and do—sin (see Rom. 7:14-24).

So, back to our question: *If Christ's forgiveness brings me into a relationship with God, what happens when I sin again?*

As believers, we still possess Christ's forgiveness even when we sin. Jesus is our Advocate before the divine court of God. He is at the right hand of God interceding on our behalf (see Rom. 8:34). This results in salvation, of course, but it also means the availability of ongoing forgiveness. In Christ, we *become* recipients of God's forgiveness, and we *remain* recipients of that forgiveness.

Earlier, I mentioned judicial forgiveness, which occurs once when God grants us salvation on the basis of the work of Christ. The second way to look at forgiveness could be called "parental forgiveness." This aspect of forgiveness is required each time we sin.

When a child is disobedient, his relationship with his parents is affected, but he does not cease to be a son. Similarly, when we fall short of obeying God, our relationship with Him remains intact. Since Christians are God's adopted children, He does not cease to be our Father, nor does He disown us—although fellowship is broken.

We can return to full fellowship with God through confession and repentance (as we saw in 1 John 1:9). Jesus is ever our Advocate, lovingly standing on our behalf. **We can be—and will be—forgiven by God each time we sin.**

How do God's character qualities (such as holiness, love, and justice) contribute to His forgiving nature?

QUESTION #4

Though Christians receive forgiveness, that doesn't mean we always feel forgiven. Three culprits are to blame for our continuing guilt and shame:

1. Satan accuses us (see Rev. 12:10).
2. Others don't forgive us.
3. We keep reminding ourselves of our past disobedience.

How can people get out from under the burden of guilt after God has forgiven them?

QUESTION #5

While the Spirit of God convicts believers of sin, His motive is to produce repentance. Since God completely forgives us, we should not allow the accusations of Satan, others, and ourselves to overshadow the truth of our good standing and forgiveness in Christ (see Rom. 8:31-34).

We can live free of those lies by living in the truth of God's forgiveness.

"There is ... a peace and rest that you may enjoy with reason and with your eyes open; having all your sins forgiven, your greatest and most aggravated transgressions blotted out as a cloud, and buried as in the depths of the sea, that they may never be found more."

—JONATHAN EDWARDS

THE POINT	*God always forgives when I truly repent.*

LIVE IT OUT

How will you respond to God's offer of forgiveness?

- **Step back for a self-evaluation.** As you pray this week, ask the Holy Spirit to reveal any areas of unconfessed sin in your life. Confess those sins in that moment.
- **Let go of false guilt.** Seek out areas in your life where you are living under false guilt for sins already forgiven. Choose to believe and accept God's offer of forgiveness.
- **Forgive when it hurts.** Be intentional about forgiving those who have wronged you—even if you don't want to. Remember that your forgiveness can point others to the ultimate forgiveness in Christ.

You've broken God's rules—a lot. But your fellowship with Him doesn't have to remain broken. Seek Him and you will find true forgiveness and full restoration.

Forgiveness and Forgetfulness

LEGACY LIVING / INVESTING IN RELATIONSHIPS

Forgiveness and Forgetfulness

By Gene A. Getz

Think what the apostle Paul must have felt during his final days. In that dark and terrible Roman dungeon, he wrote to his faithful disciple and coworker, Timothy: "At my first defense, no one stood by me, but everyone deserted me" (2 Tim. 4:16). Paul didn't explain why, but we can speculate. There were many in Rome who had come to Christ through Paul's ministry; yet, when he faced accusations by the evil Emperor Nero, many who knew about his incarceration deserted him. They were, no doubt, horribly fearful. Nevertheless, this betrayal was perhaps one of Paul's most painful experiences.

To continue reading "Forgiveness and Forgetfulness" from *Mature Living* magazine, visit *BibleStudiesforLife.com/articles.*

My group's prayer requests

My thoughts

SESSION 5

GOD IS WISE

What's the wisest advice you've ever embraced or ignored?

#BSFLwise

QUESTION #1

THE POINT

God will give me wisdom when I humbly seek it.

THE BIBLE MEETS LIFE

"Google it."

Want to learn different methods for outdoor grilling? Google it. Want to locate a good doctor in your area? Google it. Want to know fun things to do when you visit Topeka? Google it.

Search engines are great for finding information, but where do you go for wisdom? Google? I tried, and now I have access to 143 million websites about wisdom. But I don't want information *about* wisdom; I want wisdom itself.

It's easy to seek advice from other people. But true wisdom—the insight we need for effective living—only comes from God. He offers the timeless wisdom on which we can build our lives. Paul wrote in Romans 11:33 that God's wisdom is unsearchable; thankfully, He will give it to us if we ask (see Jas. 1:5).

As we'll see in this session, the Book of Proverbs points us to the beauty of God's wisdom.

WHAT DOES THE BIBLE SAY?

Proverbs 2:1-6; 3:5-7 *(HCSB)*

2:1 My son, if you accept my words and store up my commands within you,

2 listening closely to wisdom and directing your heart to understanding;

3 furthermore, if you call out to insight and lift your voice to understanding,

4 if you seek it like silver and search for it like hidden treasure,

5 then you will understand the fear of the LORD and discover the knowledge of God.

6 For the LORD gives wisdom; from His mouth come knowledge and understanding.

3:5 Trust in the LORD with all your heart, and do not rely on your own understanding;

6 think about Him in all your ways, and He will guide you on the right paths.

7 Don't consider yourself to be wise; fear the LORD and turn away from evil.

Key Words

Fear of the LORD (2:5)—Reverential awe of God because of His power and His love for us that compelled Him to provide redemption and escape from His wrath against sin.

Trust (3:5)—The Hebrew means "to be confident" or "cause to be confident." It refers to depending upon someone for safety and security. It often includes the concept of hope.

Proverbs 2:1-6

Knowledge and wisdom are not the same thing. One is information, while the other is the divinely enabled application of truth to our lives (see Col. 1:9-10). Wisdom comes only from God because God alone possesses all truth. He is the ultimate source of wisdom and knowledge (see Col. 2:3).

The truth we discover in Proverbs 2 is that God wants to impart His wisdom to us, which is why verse 4 calls us to seek His wisdom. So how do we do that?

- **Ask the right Person (Prov. 2:6).** James said if we ask God for wisdom and believe He will give it, then God will grant us wisdom (see Jas. 1:5).

- **Have the right attitude (Prov. 2:2).** Catch the emphasis in verse 2: we are to direct our hearts toward wisdom and understanding. God gives wisdom to those whose hearts are right and receptive toward Him. In other words, God expects us to do what He says.

- **Use the right tools (Prov. 2:3-4).** Get into God's Word. Wisdom must be actively pursued. It requires effort, like the hard labor of extracting silver from rock. God's Spirit will often speak to us through prayer, circumstances, and other people—but the wisdom and direction imparted by the Holy Spirit will always be consistent with Scripture.

Where in our culture do people look for wisdom?

QUESTION **#2**

God is true to His Word. If we obey His principles for seeking wisdom, He will give it to us abundantly. As God teaches us, we come to realize that: "He gives wisdom to the wise and knowledge to those who have understanding. He reveals the deep and hidden things" (Dan. 2:21-22).

How do we recognize wisdom?

QUESTION **#3**

Proverbs 3:5-6

Wisdom is the product of a real and intimate relationship with God, which means growing in wisdom is a process. Like any relationship, the more you walk with God and grow in your relationship with Him, the more you will discover His wisdom. So, the promise of God's guidance in verse 6 should not be understood as a passive trust in God; it's the by-product of thinking about Him "in all your ways."

The way to wisdom is in trusting the Lord to give the guidance needed. So, what does "trusting the Lord" look like?

- **Wait on God and His perfect timing.** Trusting God means walking in step with the Holy Spirit and patiently living on His timetable. God knows everything and is in complete control, so you can surrender the details of every situation to Him.

- **Rely on God's wisdom rather than human understanding.** Relying on God shouldn't be a passive activity. Take the time to deliberately study and meditate on God's Word in order to gain His perspective on your life.

Trust and obedience to God will result in receiving divine wisdom. The promise that God will direct your paths (v. 6) is based on the premise that you trust Him with all your heart (v. 5). Your trust is reflected in your obedience.

"Trust" (verse 5) carries the idea of prostrating yourself. It's an inward motivation to subject yourself to God and be vulnerable before Him. This is pictured in the physical act of not only kneeling in submission, but even lying face down. When you submit yourself to God in that way, you are in a position to fully hear His wisdom and receive His loving guidance.

"Now if any of you lacks wisdom, he should ask God, who gives to all generously and without criticizing, and it will be given to him."

—JAMES 1:5

Proverbs 3:7

How do you navigate the tension between trusting God's wisdom and trusting your own competence?

QUESTION #4

Many people live with an overly optimistic view of their own wisdom, which is why this verse cautions us to be wary of what we think we know. It's easy to trust our own common sense. We may even believe our motives are implicitly trustworthy and our judgments are free of bias—but we would do well to avoid such naiveté.

Wisdom is not mere common sense. It's not simply being reasonable or rational. It's not intuition, instinct, or sanctified guessing.

Wisdom is a supernatural product of divine discernment given by God through His Spirit. Considering that God Himself is the source, it's wise to trust His wisdom instead of our own.

Trusting in the Lord is not being anti-intellectual. Rational thinking has its place. After all, God created us as rational, reasoning human beings. God can—and does—use our minds. Let's never forget, though, that God's ways are above our ways, and His thoughts are above our thoughts (see Isa. 55:8-9). That's why the wise Christian fears God with holy reverence and trusts His wisdom first.

God knows everything, which is why we need His wisdom. As we seek the Lord, He is prepared at all times to give us His divine leading when we need it. But the treasure trove of wisdom that comes from Him is only for the humble, not for those who consider themselves wise by their own standards.

How can a person intentionally cultivate humility?

QUESTION #5

By disavowing our own wisdom, we resist the temptation to overestimate our insight. Conversely, when we fail to humble ourselves in this way, our sinful humanity quickly exalts itself. This creates a self-sufficiency which can lead us to elevate ourselves and reject God's authority in other areas of our lives. Ultimately, this leads to sin. Humble trust is the posture of the truly wise. Any other posture will keep us from God's wisdom—and God's best.

GOOD ADVICE?

We've all heard lots of "wisdom sayings" over the years. Think of the main sayings you've encountered and record them in the following categories.

WORLDLY WISDOM	GOOD ADVICE	BIBLICAL WISDOM
"Cleanliness is next to godliness."	"The early bird gets the worm."	"Love your neighbor as yourself."

How do we discern between good and bad advice in today's culture?

LIVE IT OUT

How will you respond to God's wisdom?

- **Memorize.** Commit James 1:5 to memory as a reminder that God grants us wisdom when we seek Him and ask for it.
- **Seek advice.** God often speaks to us through the wisdom and counsel of others. Make a connection with someone who can offer prayer and biblical counsel when you need it.
- **Immerse yourself in God's Word.** Seek wisdom by developing a long-term strategy for studying the Bible. Plan out which portions of the Bible you will study in the next 6-12 months, and identify commentaries or other additional resources that would enhance your experience.

Search, and you will find information. Seek and ask humbly, and you will find wisdom—God's wisdom. He is prepared at all times to give what you need.

Accept His Plan

Accept HIS PLAN

In the midst of a career change, God called me to accept His plan and look for unexpected fruit.

My students have been placed before me by God's design to teach, inspire, and love as God loves me.

Something seemed amiss. . . . I had been faithfully serving as a full-time music minister for 32 years. I loved my work. I was good at it. Though I had my share of struggles in church life, I had always imagined retiring as a full-time music minister. That was not to be. Arriving at a church in North Louisiana, I soon realized after eight months that the church was not happy with me, nor was I with them.

To continue reading "Accept His Plan" from *Mature Living* magazine, visit *BibleStudiesforLife.com/articles.*

My group's prayer requests

My thoughts

SESSION 6

GOD IS FAITHFUL

What comes to mind when you hear the word "guarantee"?

#BSFLfaithful

QUESTION **#1**

THE POINT

God's past faithfulness ensures our future is secure.

THE BIBLE MEETS LIFE

Promises, promises.

Have promises lost their value to you? Management promised your job wasn't in jeopardy, but now you're unemployed. A friend promised to pay you back on payday, but that was six months ago. And we all know the fickleness of a politician's campaign promise.

Even the most sincere person can't guarantee every promise, and even the best of us can become cynical. For an idea of how rare faithfulness has become, look at how society marvels when a married couple celebrates a 50th, 40th, or even a 25th anniversary.

But faithfulness is not absent in this life. We have a God who keeps His promises. God is faithful to His Word and faithful to us. Unlike everyone else, He can guarantee to keep every one of His promises.

The Book of Hebrews provides a small glimpse of how God made a promise and kept it through the centuries. Best of all: He remains faithful to that promise today.

WHAT DOES THE BIBLE SAY?

Hebrews 6:17-20; 10:19-23 *(HCSB)*

6:17 Because God wanted to show His unchangeable purpose even more clearly to the heirs of the promise, He guaranteed it with an oath,

18 so that through two unchangeable things, in which it is impossible for God to lie, we who have fled for refuge might have strong encouragement to seize the hope set before us.

19 We have this hope as an anchor for our lives, safe and secure. It enters the inner sanctuary behind the curtain.

20 Jesus has entered there on our behalf as a forerunner, because He has become a high priest forever in the order of Melchizedek.

10:19 Therefore, brothers, since we have boldness to enter the sanctuary through the blood of Jesus,

20 by a new and living way He has opened for us through the curtain (that is, His flesh),

21 and since we have a great high priest over the house of God,

22 let us draw near with a true heart in full assurance of faith, our hearts sprinkled clean from an evil conscience and our bodies washed in pure water.

23 Let us hold on to the confession of our hope without wavering, for He who promised is faithful.

Key Words

The curtain (6:19)—The veil in the temple that separated the holy of holies, where God dwelled, from the people. It was torn when Jesus died, giving all people access to God.

Forerunner (6:20)—A person who goes in front of others to lead them where they could not go on their own or to prepare the way for them.

Melchizedek (6:20)—Old Testament king/priest who blessed Abram and also received tithes from him; forerunner of the Messiah; and symbol of the inferior priestly system Jesus would surpass.

How have your experiences with human faithfulness affected the way you perceive God's faithfulness?

QUESTION **#2**

Hebrews 6:17-18

When God makes a promise, He will be faithful to keep His word. How can we know that? Look at the life of Abraham. When God first called Abraham (see Gen. 12:1-3), He promised that Abraham and his descendants would receive His blessing. God confirmed that promise years later (see Gen. 17:4-8), and when Abraham obediently offered Isaac as a sacrifice, God again confirmed His promised blessing (see Gen. 22:17-18).

God made an explicit promise of faithfulness. He did this by guaranteeing it with an oath. Keep in mind that God's "yes" means "yes," but because it's the practice of people to form binding statements to confirm agreements, God also used an oath. Doing so changed nothing about the outcome—God was always going to act faithfully, oath or not.

In the Bible, oaths are considered serious and sacred (see Deut. 10:20). Divine oaths are of a unique character, being extremely sacred and unbreakable. There are no more serious and sacred words than those of an oath. When *God* makes an oath, then, it carries the idea of the most important promise possible. God's guarantee is a formal assurance that the conditions He laid out will be fulfilled.

Despite the best intentions of reliable people, human promises are subject to being broken simply because we are finite beings. We have limited knowledge, limited power, limited presence, and limited control of a very small part of our environment. People simply cannot guarantee all their promises.

Not so with God. He is the all-in-all. He is all-knowing, all-powerful, everywhere present, completely good, and unchanging. **When God makes a promise, He will keep it.**

"When our Lord looked at us, He saw not only what we were—He was faithful in seeing what we could become!"

—A. W. TOZER

Hebrews 6:19-20; 10:19-21

Our hope in God's promise securely anchors our faith. Anchors were once symbolic within Christianity because God's promises are anchors of reliability in an unsure world. The certainty of God's promises provides an immovable anchor that can make our faith in Him unshakable.

How can God's faithfulness be an anchor?

QUESTION **#3**

When God established a covenant, it was built on a relationship with Him. For example, God entered into a covenant relationship with Abraham, which included His promise of blessing (see Heb. 6:13; Gen. 22:17-18). God also established a covenant with Moses and the entire Israelite community at Sinai (see Ex. 19–20).

That covenant provided a way for the Jews, God's chosen people, to live in relationship with God (see Ex. 24:3-8). Though the Israelites failed to honor their promise to the Lord, God promised to never break His covenant with them (see Gen. 17:7).

God's faithfulness continued as He established a new covenant through Jesus—a covenant in which He offers salvation to all people (see Heb. 9:15-26). God's promise in this new covenant brings salvation through reconciliation and intimacy with God, which is symbolized by our access into the inner sanctuary of God. This inner sanctuary is the most holy place, the holy of holies, and it represents the privileged access granted to all who surrender to God in faith and repentance to meet with God in intimate fellowship.

When has Jesus kept you anchored?

QUESTION **#4**

Jesus is the physical incarnation of God's love and the fulfillment of His covenant (see John 3:16). He established a new covenant in His blood (see Matt. 26:28). In becoming our offering for sin, Jesus entered into the holy of holies with His own blood.

The result? We now have access to God.

Hebrews 10:22-23

God has been faithful; He is faithful; and He will remain faithful. This faithfulness attests to the fact that He can be believed. Because of all God has done for us and on our behalf, He has the moral authority to ask us to trust Him. Anything less is not worthy of Him.

This passage notes two things that happen when we place our trust in the One who is faithful:

1. **Our hearts are made clean through the blood of Christ.** God's salvation means we receive His righteousness; it is imputed to us through His work.

2. **Our bodies are washed in pure water.** The water mentioned in verse 22 represents the symbolic washing away of our sins through immersion (i.e., baptism) in the Holy Spirit (see Rom. 6:3-5). The Bible often uses the imagery of water to describe the Holy Spirit (see John 7:37-39). Therefore, being baptized in water serves as a public statement of our faith in Christ and a firm testimony to others.

Baptism in New Testament times was an extreme and sober act of faith. Because Christians were being persecuted, being immersed as a statement of faith was a clear indicator of a person's unwavering confidence in Christ. According to the writer of Hebrews, this is exactly what God wants—believers who hold on to a confession of their hope without wavering.

God expects His faithfulness to be reciprocated. He who promised us is faithful. And just as we can fully trust Him, we are to remain faithful to Him. God want us to draw near to Him with a true heart and to be fully committed to Him—just as He is fully committed to us. God wants us to know Him like He knows us. When we do so, our faith will become unshakable.

How can we help each other draw near to God and hold on to our hope?

QUESTION **#5**

YOUR STORY

Use the space below to record a time when God demonstrated His faithfulness to you. Get creative by telling a story, sketching a picture, making a list, writing a poem, and so on.

LIVE IT OUT

In light of God's faithfulness, how should you respond?

- **Seek out God's promises.** As you read God's Word, highlight any verses that contain a promise from Him.
- **Remember God's faithfulness.** Find a picture of an anchor (or draw one yourself) and display it someplace you'll see it every day. Let the image remind you that God's faithfulness is an anchor for your life.
- **Fulfill your promises.** Take a step back and evaluate the different promises you've made in recent months. If there are any promises you've yet to keep, move forward to reconcile the situation.

Place your future in Christ's hands and walk with Him in the present. He is faithful in this life and the next. That's a promise you can count on for all time.

Moving Mountains

Moving Mountains

BY RACHEL DAVIS

"Dear Ms. Parks. This is Arianna Miskowski. I am in Ms. Dubois' class. I found out in Sunday School that kids in Haiti have to play with parts of old cars for toys. This made me sad. I don't have money, but I have a lot of stuffed animals I don't play with anymore. I know my classmates probably do also. I was thinking I could collect them all for the kids in Haiti. My mom said she could wash and dry them and help me get them to Haiti through our church. Would it be OK if I asked the kids to bring me the stuffed animals they don't play with anymore? Can you help me with my idea? Sincerely, Arianna Miskowski."

To continue reading "Moving Mountains" from *Mature Living* magazine, visit *BibleStudiesforLife.com/articles*.

My group's prayer requests

My thoughts

Beyond Belief: Exploring the Character of God

Our study during the last few weeks has shown us that what we know about God moves beyond just belief; it moves us to know Him. We are moved to live fruitful lives in right relationship with Him.

Christ

Jesus Christ is the exact expression of the nature and character of God (see Heb. 1:3). To understand how God displays His holiness, love, justice, forgiveness, wisdom, and faithfulness, we look at the life and ministry of Christ.

Community

As Christ indwells believers through His Holy Spirit, we reflect His holiness, love, justice, forgiveness, wisdom, and faithfulness. As the body of Christ, we are not to point to ourselves. Our interaction with each other and with the world around us should reflect the nature and character of God.

Culture

The world around us sees God's love when we act in love. The world sees God's justice when we, as His representatives, work for justice. The world sees the true nature of God when the church steps out into the world to live as Christ.

LEADER GUIDE BEYOND BELIEF

GENERAL INSTRUCTIONS

In order to make the most of this study and to ensure a richer group experience, it's recommended that all group participants read through the teaching and discussion content in full before each group meeting. As a leader, it is also a good idea for you to be familiar with this content and prepared to summarize it for your group members as you move through the material each week.

Each session of the Bible study is made up of three sections:

1. THE BIBLE MEETS LIFE.

An introduction to the theme of the session and its connection to everyday life, along with a brief overview of the primary Scripture text. This section also includes an icebreaker question or activity.

2. WHAT DOES THE BIBLE SAY?

This comprises the bulk of each session and includes the primary Scripture text along with explanations for key words and ideas within that text. This section also includes most of the content designed to produce and maintain discussion within the group.

3. LIVE IT OUT.

The final section focuses on application, using bulleted summary statements to answer the question, *So what?* As the leader, be prepared to challenge the group to apply what they learned during the discussion by transforming it into action throughout the week.

For group leaders, the *Beyond Belief* leader guide contains several features and tools designed to help you lead participants through the material provided.

QUESTION 1: ICEBREAKER

These opening questions and/or activities are designed to help participants transition into the study and begin engaging the primary themes to be discussed. Be sure everyone has a chance to speak, but maintain a low-pressure environment.

DISCUSSION QUESTIONS

Each "What Does the Bible Say?" section features at least four questions designed to spark discussion and interaction within your group. These questions encourage critical thinking, so be sure to allow a period of silence for participants to process the question and form an answer.

The *Beyond Belief* leader guide also contains follow-up questions and optional activities that may be helpful to your group, if time permits.

DVD CONTENT

Each video features Freddy Cardoza teaching about the primary themes found in the session. We recommend that you show this video in one of three places: (1) At the beginning of group time, (2) After the icebreaker, or (3) After a quick review and/or summary of "What Does the Bible Say?" A video summary is included as well. You may choose to use this summary as background preparation to help you guide the group.

The leader guide contains additional questions to help unpack the video and transition into the discussion. For a digital leader guide with commentary, see the "Leader Tools" folder on the DVD-ROM in your Bible study kit.

SESSION 1: GOD IS HOLY

The Point: God's holiness calls me to be holy.

The Passage: Psalm 99:1-9

The Setting: The holiness and sovereignty of God is the theme of Psalm 99. The psalm can be divided into three divisions, and each division concludes with the exclamation of God's holiness. Psalm 99 not only declares the holiness of God, but it describes His holiness in light of His righteous and just character. The psalm shows us how God demonstrates His holiness. As one of the enthronement psalms (see Pss. 93–100), it affirms God's rule over the earth.

QUESTION 1: When have you seen or experienced something you would describe as one-of-a-kind?

> ***Optional activity:*** Print out descriptions of rare (one-of-a-kind) items from Sotheby's or another auction house. Post these descriptions on the wall or pass them around to group members to enhance the discussion. If time allows, consider asking the following questions:
>
> - Which of these items do you like best? Why?
> - In your opinion, which one seems least valuable?
> - When have you seen or experienced something you would describe as one-of-a-kind? (Note: This question is the same as the question 1. If you use the optional activity, ask this question last rather than first.)

Video Summary: In this video message Freddy talks about God's holiness and how this fundamental biblical truth helps us know and understand God. We can't know God and accurately understand what He is doing in our lives and in the world without understanding His holiness. Freddy also speaks of two truths related to God's holiness—His transcendence and His immanence. *Transcendence* means that God is separate from and above all creation. There is nothing or no one like Him. *Immanence* means that though He is holy, God is also intimately involved in our everyday lives. So, what does His holiness mean for us? It means we can trust Him and trust that He is working in and through our lives.

WATCH THE DVD SEGMENT FOR SESSION 1. THEN USE THE FOLLOWING QUESTIONS AND DISCUSSION POINTS TO TRANSITION INTO THE STUDY.

- In what ways does understanding God's holiness motivate you to pursue holiness in your own life?
- In his video message Freddy says, "God always acts in accordance with who He is. And who He is never changes." As it relates to holiness, what implications do you think this truth should have on the way you live out your life day to day?

WHAT DOES THE BIBLE SAY?

ASK FOR A VOLUNTEER TO READ ALOUD PSALM 99:1-9.

Response: What's your initial reaction to these verses?

- What do you like about the text?
- What questions do you have about these verses?

TURN THE GROUP'S ATTENTION TO PSALM 99:1-3.

QUESTION 2: When was a time God's holiness became real to you?

This question gives group members an opportunity to share specific spiritual markers from their lives. It utilizes the value of storytelling while advancing the group discussion on God's holiness at the same time.

> ***Optional follow-up based on Luke 5:1-11:*** What emotions do you experience when you are in God's presence?

> ***Optional activity:*** Direct group members to complete the "Picturing Holiness" activity on page 9. If time permits, ask for volunteers to share which images they selected and explain how they would strive for holiness in that area.

MOVE TO PSALM 99:4-5.

QUESTION 3: How does God's justice, fairness, or righteousness impact your daily routine?

Because notions of justice, fairness, and righteousness are words with tremendous impact, we often do not consider the ways these aspects of God's character impact our day-to-day, minute-to-minute lives. Challenge the group to think about how God's holiness should be more of a regular part of even the most mundane events and moments.

> ***Optional follow-up:*** How often do you feel the impact of God's justice, fairness, or righteousness?

CONTINUE WITH PSALM 99:6-9.

QUESTION 4: What do these verses teach us about a lifestyle of worship?

Interpretation questions ask group members to consider how they will integrate the biblical truth into their lives. Because the text cites God's holiness as worthy of our exaltation, group members are being asked here to discuss the hows and whys of a constant posture of worship and how this posture moves us toward personal holiness.

> ***Optional follow-up:*** In what ways can you cultivate a heart of reverent worship in response to God's holiness?

QUESTION 5: How can we tremble at God's holiness yet still have an intimate relationship with Him?

Group members are asked again to discuss the ways we can navigate the tension inherent in a God that is both near and far, both demanding taskmaster and sacrificial lamb, embodying both perfect justice and perfect grace. Answers to questions like these often reveal what we really believe isn't what we think we believe.

> ***Optional follow-up:*** How can we support each other in our efforts to grow closer with God?

Note: The following question does not appear in the Bible study book. Use it in your group discussion as time allows.

QUESTION 6: What steps can you take this week to increase your exposure to (or awareness of) God's holiness?

Ending group time with an application question should leave group members with a sense of action. Drive this point home before you dismiss.

LIVE IT OUT

God's holiness is not an abstract concept with no practical impact on how we live. We are called to be holy because God is holy (see 1 Pet. 1:16). Invite group members to consider these practical ways to live a life of holiness:

- **Surrender.** Submit to God's holiness by placing your faith in Christ for salvation.
- **Bow in worship.** Be intentional about praising God this week. Set aside a specific period of time and worship Him in response to His holiness.
- **Unplug and listen.** Choose to abstain from one form of technology this week—social media, texts, TV, and so on. Use that time each day as an opportunity to focus on God.

Challenge: Spend some time this week reflecting on Ephesians 2:10. Consider what it means that we are products of God's personal attention and handiwork as it relates to His holiness.

Pray: Ask for prayer requests and ask group members to pray for the different requests as intercessors. As the leader, close this time by committing the members of your group to the Lord and asking Him to convict the hearts of everyone present regarding the importance of His holiness and its implications in your lives.

SESSION 2: GOD IS LOVING

The Point: God's love empowers me to love.

The Passage: 1 John 4:7-12

The Setting: The apostle John wrote this letter to encourage believers, to lead them to avoid sin and false teaching, and to help them know they have eternal life. The topic of love permeates this short book, leading us to focus on the love of God and our need to love one another. One of the evidences that we have a relationship with God is the presence and demonstration of His love in our lives.

QUESTION 1: What makes you love someone?

Optional activity: Supplement the point of this session by asking group members to list things they encounter in their everyday lives that give power. As a visual reminder, consider listing their contributions on a white board or tear sheet. Encourage participants to remind themselves of how God's love empowers us to love others as they use the items listed throughout the week.

Video Summary: In this video message Freddy talks about a love that is far beyond all intimate loves—the love of God. God made us with a unique capacity for emotions, passions, meaning, and purpose. He made us with a need to give and receive love so that our hunger for love would lead us to pursue a relationship with Him. Everything God does is motivated by love. Jesus' death and resurrection proves that absolutely nothing can keep God from loving us. But God doesn't love us just so we can keep that love to ourselves. He wants us to give that love away. We are never more like Him than when we love others.

WATCH THE DVD SEGMENT FOR SESSION 2. THEN USE THE FOLLOWING QUESTIONS AND DISCUSSION POINTS TO TRANSITION INTO THE STUDY.

- Freddy spends a lot of time talking about how we were created with a fundamental need to be loved and with unique capacities for emotions, meaning, and purpose. As it relates to God's attribute of love, why do you think these things matter?
- How does God's love empower you to love others?

WHAT DOES THE BIBLE SAY?

ASK FOR A VOLUNTEER TO READ ALOUD 1 JOHN 4:7-12.

Response: What's your initial reaction to these verses?

- What questions do you have about these verses?
- What application do you hope to gain about how God empowers us to love others?

TURN THE GROUP'S ATTENTION TO 1 JOHN 4:7-8.

QUESTION 2: How does the statement "God is love" differ from saying "God loves"?

Taking a familiar phrase and putting a little twist on it can be a good way to begin group discussion. This approach can contribute to an environment where minds are more open to fresh understanding of even established biblical truths.

Optional activity: Direct group members to complete the "Power to Love" activity on page 19. Invite volunteers to share their responses to the final question: What can you learn by comparing both measurements?

MOVE TO 1 JOHN 4:9-10.

QUESTION 3: What do you find remarkable in verses 9-10?

Examine 1 John 4:7-10 closely as a group to engage this question at the most effective level. This may mean reading and re-reading the passage, circling prominent words, or sharing the commentary found on the DVD-ROM. You'll want to fully unpack a word we use multiple times every day: *love.*

Optional follow-up: How would you describe the meaning of the word *propitiation?*

QUESTION 4: When have you sensed God's love and power at work in your life?

Group members should continue the discussion from the previous question and apply a deeper understanding of love here. Be prepared for those who might struggle answering this question, as well as nonbelievers. Don't be afraid of silence.

Optional follow-up: How have you been changed or influenced by God's love and power?

CONTINUE WITH 1 JOHN 4:11-12.

QUESTION 5: How will being loved by God shape the way you live?

Ensure an adequate understanding of the text prior to engaging this application question. This is also a good place in the group time to re-state the point of this session for everyone.

Optional follow-up: What obstacles can prevent us from responding to God's love?

Note: The following question does not appear in the Bible study book. Use it in your group discussion as time allows.

QUESTION 6: What are some specific ways you can choose to love others this week?

Ending group time with an application question should leave group members with a sense of action. Encourage group members to be specific in answering. This may mean writing or naming names.

LIVE IT OUT

Direct group member to consider these three ways God's love can shape their day-to-day lives.

- **Embrace God's love.** Pray specifically for God to help you understand, believe, and receive His love for you today.
- **Reflect God's love.** Before the day is over, make an effort to express love to someone in a way that mirrors God's love for you. (Note: this experience will be most powerful if you're able to express love to someone who doesn't deserve it.)
- **Seek reconciliation.** Identify a relationship that's been strained or broken in recent years. Let God's empowering love be the catalyst for you to request or offer forgiveness in that relationship as a step toward reconciliation.

Challenge: Great leaders rarely stand alone. There is a power that motivates and influences *your* actions and behavior as well—friends, an employer, a spouse, or even the sway of the crowd or a slick marketing message. Spend some time this week thinking about where you choose to draw your power to reflect His love.

Pray: Ask for prayer requests and ask group members to pray for the requests as intercessors. Encourage them to speak with God—silently or out loud—regarding their responsibility to reflect His love to those around them.

SESSION 3: GOD IS JUST

The Point: God is always just.

The Passage: Ezekiel 18:21-24,30-32

The Setting: The prophet Ezekiel ministered during some of the darkest days of Israel's history: the destruction of Jerusalem and the temple by the Babylonians and the subsequent exile of the people. Chapter 18 addresses the responsibility of all the people to respond to the message of the Lord. God is just and does not allow the righteousness or unrighteousness of one person to dictate another person's relationship with Him.

QUESTION 1: When it comes to fighting for justice, who is your favorite character?

> ***Optional activity:*** Help group members connect with the concept of justice by providing them with a small example of injustice. Show a quick clip from a movie (or read a brief excerpt from a book) in which characters are treated unfairly.

Video Summary: This week Freddy talks about how a distorted view of justice can undermine our trust in God. In Ezekiel 18:21-24,30-32 we see that the Jews were confused about why the Babylonians seemed to be prospering while God's chosen nation was experiencing defeat. The Jews made the common mistake of assuming God was either not fair or not good. But what we see in these verses is that the Babylonians had regrets and repented while the Jews were relying on their privileged position and past spiritual heritage rather than a right relationship with God.

WATCH THE DVD SEGMENT FOR SESSION 3. THEN USE THE FOLLOWING QUESTIONS AND DISCUSSION POINTS TO TRANSITION INTO THE STUDY.

- Freddy opens his video teaching by saying that justice "may be one of the most misunderstood and troublesome parts of God's character." In your opinion, why is this the case?
- In what ways do you think having a distorted view of justice can undermine our trust in God?

WHAT DOES THE BIBLE SAY?

ASK FOR A VOLUNTEER TO READ ALOUD EZEKIEL 18:21-24,30-32.

Response: What's your initial reaction to these verses?

- What questions do you have about these verses?
- What new application do you hope to get from this passage?

TURN THE GROUP'S ATTENTION TO EZEKIEL 18:21-23.

QUESTION 2: Why does it sometimes bother us when someone gets let off the hook?

This type of question is good for self examination. This discussion is not meant to be incriminating or to indict anyone; rather, it's an opportunity to be candid and honest about the human condition and our sinfulness.

> ***Optional follow-up based on Jonah 4:1-3:*** Do you think it is appropriate to root for worldly people to receive judgment? Explain.

MOVE TO EZEKIEL 18:24.

QUESTION 3: How do these verses serve as both good news and bad news?

It may be helpful to broaden the scope to include verses 22-23. God's justice has nothing to do with time (when we make a decision for Jesus) and everything to do with repentance (sincerity of the heart). The good news is that it's never too late. The bad news is that we're accountable to God, who is always just.

> ***Optional follow-up:*** What emotions do you experience when you read verses 21-24?

QUESTION 4: Why don't we take sin as seriously as we should?

Challenge the group to answer from their own experience. It's easy to talk about why someone else doesn't take sin seriously. It's wise, however, not to emphasize to such a point that it stalls group participation.

CONTINUE WITH EZEKIEL 18:30-32.

QUESTION 5: God is both just and forgiving. How does that combination lead to a full life for those who follow Him?

It's difficult to comprehend a God that is perfectly just but also totally forgiving, yet God is both at the same time. The challenge is to put aside our either/or mentality in favor of both/and. Living in the reality of a God that is both/and is a demanding pursuit that is innately fulfilling.

> ***Optional activity:*** Encourage group members to complete the "What Do You Say?" activity on page 31. Allow them to work in silence for three to five minutes. If time permits, encourage volunteers to share their responses.

Note: The following question does not appear in the Bible study book. Use it in your group discussion as time allows.

QUESTION 6: How does God's justice impact or influence your relationship with Him?

This question is self-revelation in nature. It asks group members to be open in discussing how they are doing in light of the fact that God is always just.

Optional follow-up: How is God's attribute of justice both a comfort and challenge for believers?

LIVE IT OUT

Encourage group members to examine these three ways to respond to God's justice:

- **Choose freedom.** Confess a specific sin or sinful pattern to God. Receive His forgiveness and choose to move forward with the knowledge that He has set you free from that sin.
- **Seek justice in the world.** Look for situations where justice seems to be lacking. Use these situations as reminders to pray that God would carry out His justice in the world.
- **Close the gap between your reputation and character.** Ask a fellow believer to hold you accountable in areas where you struggle with sin. Commit to integrity between how others know you and how God knows you.

Challenge: As you go through this next week, be on the lookout for times when you feel you are being or have been treated unfairly. Before reacting to the situation and trying to handle things yourself, remember that God is always just and He always delivers. The approach God takes is always perfectly appropriate.

Pray: Ask for prayer requests and ask members to pray for the different requests as intercessors. As the leader, close this time by asking the Lord to give each of you strength and courage to confess that He is always just and to speak with Him about the consequences of His justice in connection with the different aspects of your lives.

SESSION 4: GOD IS FORGIVING

The Point: God always forgives when I truly repent.

The Passage: 1 John 1:5–2:2

The Setting: The apostle John wrote the Letter of 1 John to believers facing the attack of their faith by false teachers. He wrote to counteract the doctrinal, moral, and social fabrications proclaimed by those misguided teachers and to assure believers of the trustworthiness of the gospel they had first received. He included in his reassurance the reality that every person sins, but Christ's work provides the means of restored fellowship with God.

QUESTION 1: What rule did you break the most growing up?

Optional activity: Supplement the point of this session by bringing a hand-held mirror to the gathering. Ask each person who shares during the group discussion to hold the mirror as a reminder that any conversation about forgiveness must start with our own need to be forgiven.

Video Summary: This week's video message focuses on a message from John (1 John 1:5–2:2) about a concept he knew well—God's forgiveness. Forgiveness is an enormous issue in our world today because it has to do with relationships and the breaking of trust. We were created to live in relationship with God and others. Forgiveness matters because relationships matter. Forgiveness establishes our relationship with God at the moment of salvation and then reestablishes fellowship with Him for the rest of our lives on an ongoing basis. Reconciliation—at the moment of salvation and throughout our lives—brings fellowship with God and then fellowship with others. Forgiveness is always available to us—Christ has the power to change lives.

WATCH THE DVD SEGMENT FOR SESSION 4. THEN USE THE FOLLOWING QUESTIONS AND DISCUSSION POINTS TO TRANSITION INTO THE STUDY.

- Freddy shares that "we can be forgiven but not feel forgiven." Why do you think it's sometimes so easy to give in to our emotions rather than believe God's truth?
- How does it make you feel to know that God never intended for us to live under false guilt or accusation?

WHAT DOES THE BIBLE SAY?

ASK FOR A VOLUNTEER TO READ ALOUD 1 JOHN 1:5–2:2.

Response: What's your initial reaction to these verses?

- What do you like about the text?
- What new application do you hope to receive about God's offer of total forgiveness?

TURN THE GROUP'S ATTENTION TO 1 JOHN 1:5-10.

QUESTION 2: What evidence do you see of darkness and light in your town or community?

Filter all discussion through the lens of 1 John 1:5-10—specifically where fellowship with God may be evident or apparently void. Experiencing forgiveness is paramount to understanding this component of God's makeup.

> ***Optional follow-up:*** What evidence do you see of darkness and light in our culture as a whole?

QUESTION 3: What emotions do you experience at the thought of confessing your sin?

You'll want to compare the responses to this question with the truth stated in the point of this session. Answers will most likely run the gamut from shame and guilt to relief. Regardless, the end result is God's forgiveness. Quite different from some common perceptions of God, "forgiving" is simply who He is.

> ***Optional activity:*** Direct participants to complete the "Barriers to Forgiveness" activity on page 39. Allow group members to share any recommended steps for knocking down barriers to forgiveness.

MOVE TO 1 JOHN 2:1-2.

QUESTION 4: How do God's character qualities (such as holiness, love, and justice) contribute to His forgiving nature?

This question is included to prompt the group to consider the totality of God's Personhood. His character qualities are bigger than any one of us or anything we could possibly do. You may stimulate discussion by revisiting or naming the many facets of His character.

> ***Optional follow-up:*** What are some different ways people define the concept of forgiveness?

QUESTION 5: How can people get out from under the burden of guilt after God has forgiven them?

This presents an opportunity to review the spiritual disciplines with a special emphasis on worship. When all else fails or seems unsure, an appropriate response to God can always be reading the Bible, prayer, or worship.

> ***Optional follow-up:*** Why do we often tolerate guilt and shame after our sins have been forgiven?

Note: The following question does not appear in the Bible study book. Use it in your group discussion as time allows.

QUESTION 6: How can we lift up the value of repentance as a group?

Focus on ways the group can give greater value, prominence, or repentance as a group. One way may be celebrating decisions of individual group members. Another way may be arranging opportunities to engage in spiritual conversations as a group.

LIVE IT OUT

Encourage group members to consider these three ways they can respond to God's offer of forgiveness:

- **Step back for a self-evaluation.** As you pray this week, ask the Holy Spirit to reveal any areas of unconfessed sin in your life. Confess those sins in that moment.
- **Let go of false guilt.** Seek out areas in your life where you are living under false guilt for sins already forgiven. Choose to believe and accept God's offer of forgiveness.
- **Forgive when it hurts.** Be intentional about forgiving those who have wronged you—even if you don't want to. Remember that your forgiveness can point others to the ultimate forgiveness in Christ.

Challenge: Study Romans 5:6-11 this week and reflect on the sacrifices that have been made for us—God has forgiven us. He forgives us when we walk away. He forgives us when we squander and abuse all He has given us. He forgives us when we hurt those He loves. Consider how much more, then, we should forgive others.

Pray: Ask for prayer requests and ask group members to pray for the different requests as intercessors. As the leader, close this time by confessing to God that all people have broken God's rules—including everyone in your group. Thank God for His continuing offer of forgiveness and fellowship.

SESSION 5: GOD IS WISE

The Point: God will give me wisdom when I humbly seek it.

The Passage: Proverbs 2:1-6; 3:5-7

The Setting: Bible students have designated the Book of Proverbs as wisdom literature. The words *wisdom, wise,* or variations of those words appear more than one hundred times in the book, clearly justifying the designation. Chapters 2 and 3 are part of a larger section in which Solomon undertakes his parental responsibility to instruct his son (see 2:1; 3:1) in wisdom and the ways of the Lord. He specifically emphasized that true wisdom comes only from the Lord.

QUESTION 1: What's the wisest advice you've ever embraced or ignored?

Optional activity: Challenge group members with portable devices to participate in a modern version of a sword drill. See who can be the first to answer the following questions using their preferred search engine:

- What plants are mentioned in Isaiah 44:4? (Answer: grass and poplars)
- What is the circumference of the Earth at the equator? (Answer: 24,901.55 miles)
- Which country has the larger population: Sweden or the Netherlands? (Answer: the Netherlands)

Video Summary: Freddy explains how knowledge and wisdom are different. Knowledge is factual information. Wisdom is the application of God's divine truth. He promises us wisdom, but how do we get that wisdom? First, by having the right attitude—a teachable heart (vv. 1-2). And second, by taking the right actions—actively pursuing wisdom rather than passively hoping for it (vv. 3-4). Wisdom is about knowing God intimately.

WATCH THE DVD SEGMENT FOR SESSION 5. THEN USE THE FOLLOWING QUESTIONS AND DISCUSSION POINTS TO TRANSITION INTO THE STUDY.

- Freddy shares, "Wise people trust in the Lord more than ..." How would you complete this statement as it refers to how you pursue God's wisdom for your own life?
- On a scale of 1 to 10, how teachable is your heart? How actively are you pursuing God's wisdom?

WHAT DOES THE BIBLE SAY?

ASK FOR A VOLUNTEER TO READ ALOUD PROVERBS 2:1-6; 3:5-7.

Response: What's your initial reaction to these verses?

- What questions do you have about these verses?
- What new application do you hope to get from this passage?

TURN THE GROUP'S ATTENTION TO PROVERBS 2:1-6.

QUESTION 2: Where in our culture do people look for wisdom?

This may be a place to compare and contrast the wisdom described in Proverbs 2:1-6 with the many options for wisdom the world around us understands as valid sources.

> ***Optional follow-up:*** Where do you typically turn when you need wisdom or advice? Why?

MOVE TO PROVERBS 3:5-6.

QUESTION 3: How do we recognize wisdom?

The text directs us not to trust our "own understanding" but rather "think about Him" when wisdom in any situation is required. But if we're not trusting ourselves, then, how are we supposed to recognize wisdom? This interpretation question asks for an honest interaction with Proverbs 3:5-6.

> ***Optional follow-up:*** How would you describe the difference between wisdom and information?

> ***Optional activity:*** Ask group members to "Good Advice?" on page 51. Encourage them to call out the main wisdom sayings they've heard and then categorize them as well as those called out by others.

CONTINUE WITH PROVERBS 3:7.

QUESTION 4: How do you navigate the tension between trusting God's wisdom and trusting your own competence?

This question asks group members to apply their interpretation of the previous question in light of verse 7. Reconnect to the point for this session by asking the group what it means to humbly seek godly wisdom.

> ***Optional follow-up:*** How can we discern when God is using others to guide us in the right direction?

QUESTION 5: How can a person intentionally cultivate humility?

Answers will vary. The objective in this question is to help group members avoid elements of pride in their humility so that they may grow in Christlikeness and in their understanding of Who God is.

Note: The following question does not appear in the Bible study book. Use it in your group discussion as time allows.

QUESTION 6: What obstacles have prevented you from seeking wisdom in the past?

Self-revelation questions ask the group to discuss how they're doing in light of a particular biblical principal or mandate. Asking about obstacles (1) identifies habits, compulsions, or erroneous conclusions that stand in the way of greater spiritual maturity; and (2) identifies prayer needs within the redemptive community.

> ***Optional follow-up:*** What steps can you take to overcome these obstacles in the future?

LIVE IT OUT

Direct group members to consider these options for responding to God's wisdom:

- **Memorize.** Commit James 1:5 to memory as a reminder that God grants us wisdom when we seek Him and ask for it.
- **Seek advice.** God often speaks to us through the wisdom and counsel of others. Make a connection with someone who can offer prayer and biblical counsel when you need it.
- **Immerse yourself in God's Word.** Seek wisdom by developing a long-term strategy for studying the Bible. Plan out which portions of the Bible you will study in the next 6 to 12 months and identify commentaries or other additional resources that would enhance your experience.

Challenge: In this session we have considered where to go for true godly wisdom, how to discern godly wisdom, and various avenues the Lord uses to speak wisdom and counsel into our lives. Spend some time this week thinking about ways you can better position yourself to be used by God to speak wisdom into the life of another.

Pray: Ask for prayer requests and ask group members to pray for the different requests as intercessors. As the leader, close this time by affirming God's promise to give wisdom when we ask for it in a humble way. Also affirm your desire to receive and act in wisdom, both for you as an individual and for your entire group.

SESSION 6: GOD IS FAITHFUL

The Point: God's past faithfulness ensures our future is secure.

The Passage: Hebrews 6:17-20; 10:19-23

The Setting: The Book of Hebrews addresses an audience made up at least in part of Jewish believers, perhaps including some of the many priests who had converted to the faith (see Acts 6:7). With time, some of these believers began to struggle with the adequacy of the gospel versus their deep-seated Jewish rituals. The writer of Hebrews sought to exhort, instruct, and reassure these believers in their faith.

QUESTION 1: What comes to mind when you hear the word "guarantee"?

> ***Optional activity:*** Bring several magazines and/or newspapers to the gathering and distribute one copy to each group members. Ask everyone to search their periodical for promises and guarantees. After three to five minutes use the following questions to unpack the experience:

- What were some of the more interesting or outrageous promises you found?
- How confident are you that such promises will be kept?
- How have these kinds of promises and guarantees influenced your ability to trust others?
- How have they influenced your ability to trust God?

Video Summary: We live in a world of overpromising and under-delivering. But God always does what He says He will do. No exceptions, no excuses. And God's past faithfulness ensures His future faithfulness. This truth is well illustrated in this week's focal passage—Hebrews 6:17-20; 10:19-23. Even though the Jews walked away from the original covenant made in Sinai, God remained faithful. But the Jews were nervous that because they hadn't been faithful, God wouldn't be faithful either. So He made an oath with them (v. 17). God didn't need to make an oath to ensure He fulfilled His promises. He did it for the Jews. And today He does it for us through the new covenant—a commitment to reconciliation and intimacy with Him through Jesus.

WATCH THE DVD SEGMENT FOR SESSION 6. THEN USE THE FOLLOWING QUESTIONS AND DISCUSSION POINTS TO TRANSITION INTO THE STUDY.

- Share a time when you overpromised and under-delivered. How did you handle the situation?
- In what ways has God's past faithfulness given you hope for present circumstances? Be specific.

WHAT DOES THE BIBLE SAY?

ASK FOR A VOLUNTEER TO READ ALOUD HEBREWS 6:17-20; 10:19-23.

Response: What's your initial reaction to these verses?

- What questions do you have about God's faithfulness?
- What new application do you hope to get from this passage?

TURN THE GROUP'S ATTENTION TO HEBREWS 6:17-18.

QUESTION 2: How have your experiences with human faithfulness affected the way you perceive God's faithfulness?

Identifying crucial elements in a person's life journey is important to how they understand God. Questions like this help us understand ourselves better which, in turn, help us understand how God works in our lives.

> ***Optional follow-up:*** What are some different ways of understanding the word *faithful*?

MOVE TO HEBREWS 6:19-20; 10:19-21.

QUESTION 3: How can God's faithfulness be an anchor?

This question asks group members to interpret Hebrews 6:19-20 and 10:19-21 for themselves as a way to move toward life application.

> ***Optional follow-up:*** What are some tangible ways you have found more courage because of God's faithfulness to His promises?

QUESTION 4: When has Jesus kept you anchored?

Be sensitive to non-Christians and those who might not be able to offer an immediate answer. Either be prepared to share yourself or ask another group member to be prepared to initiate discussion here.

Optional follow-up: What emotions do you experience when you think about the ways Jesus has kept you anchored?

Optional activity: Encourage participants to complete the "Your Story" activity on page 61. If time permits, allow volunteers to share their work and what it means.

CONTINUE WITH HEBREWS 10:22-23.

QUESTION 5: How can we help each other draw near to God and hold onto our hope?

This question is associated with building biblical community. Helping one another draw from God's promise of faithfulness is indicative of the kind of community described in Acts 2. Belonging to redemptive community is an important aspect of living life with a secure future in God's faithfulness.

Optional follow-up: What might it look like for us to demonstrate faithfulness within this group?

Note: The following question does not appear in the Bible study book. Use it in your group discussion as time allows.

QUESTION 6: What practices will help you remember and benefit from each instance of God's faithfulness?

Don't settle for pat or "usual suspect" answers here. Instead, challenge the group to be specific and intentional in building a plan for remembering and benefitting from God's faithfulness.

LIVE IT OUT

Invite group members to consider these three options for how they can respond in light of God's faithfulness:

- **Seek out God's promises.** As you read God's Word, highlight any verses that contain a promise from Him.
- **Remember God's faithfulness.** Find a picture of an anchor (or draw one yourself) and display it someplace you'll see it every day. Let the image remind you that God's faithfulness is an anchor for your life.
- **Fulfill your promises.** Take a step back and evaluate the different promises you've made in recent months. If there are any promises you've yet to keep, move forward to reconcile the situation.

Challenge: Sometimes we aren't as faithful to others as we want or ought to be. And sometimes the faithfulness of others seems totally lost to us. But faithfulness is not absent in this life. We have a God who keeps His promises. He is faithful to His Word and faithful to us. Unlike everyone else, He can guarantee to keep every one of His promises. Look for opportunities this week to live out His faithfulness by showing faithfulness to someone else.

Pray: As the leader, close this final session of *Beyond Belief* in prayer. Ask the Lord to help each of you as you move forward to be reminded daily of Who He is and how He has revealed Himself to us through Scripture.

Note: If you haven't discussed it earlier, decide as a group whether or not you plan to continue to meet together and, if so, what Bible study options you would like to pursue. Visit *LifeWay.com/smallgroups* for help, or if you would like more studies like this one, visit *biblestudiesforlife.com/smallgroups.*

WHERE THE BIBLE MEETS LIFE

Bible Studies for Life™ will help you know Christ, live in community, and impact the world around you. If you enjoyed this study, be sure and check out these other available titles.* Six sessions each.

Pressure Points *by Chip Henderson*
When Relationships Collide *by Ron Edmondson*
Do Over: Experience New Life in Christ *by Ben Mandrell*
Honest to God: Real Questions People Ask *by Robert Jeffress*
Let Hope In *by Pete Wilson*
Productive: Finding Joy in What We Do *by Ronnie and Nick Floyd*
Connected: My Life in the Church *by Thom S. Rainer*
Resilient Faith: Standing Strong in the Midst of Suffering *by Mary Jo Sharp*
Beyond Belief: Exploring the Character of God *by Freddy Cardoza*

If your group meets regularly, you might consider Bible Studies for Life as an ongoing series. Available for your entire church—kids, students, and adults—it's a format that will be a more affordable option over time. And you can jump in anytime. For more information, visit **biblestudiesforlife.com**.

biblestudiesforlife.com/smallgroups
800.458.2772 | LifeWay Christian Stores

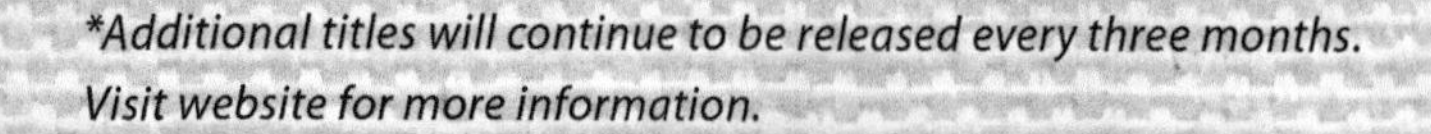